A World of Field Trips

Going to a Concert

Rebecca Rissman

Heinemann Library
Chicago, Illinois

www.capstonepub.com
Visit our website to find out more information about Heinemann-Raintree books.

To order:

☎ Phone 888-454-2279
Visit www.capstonepub.com to browse our catalog and order online.

an imprint of Capstone Global Library, LLC
Chicago, Illinois

Edited by Rebecca Rissman, Dan Nunn, and Catherine Veitch
Designed by Richard Parker
Picture research by Tracy Cummins
Originated by Capstone Global Library Ltd
Printed and bound in the United States of America in North Mankato, MN. 062013 007580RP

15 14 13
10 9 8 7 6 5 4 3

Library of Congress Cataloging-in-Publication Data
Rissman, Rebecca.
Going to a concert / Rebecca Rissman.
p. cm.—(A world of field trips)
Includes bibliographical references and index.
ISBN 978-1-4329-6065-0 (hb)—ISBN 978-1-4329-6074-2 (pb)
1. School field trips—Juvenile literature. 2. Concerts—Juvenile literature. I. Title.
LB1047.R572 2010
371.3'8—dc22 2011015047

Acknowledgments
We would like to thank the following for permission to reproduce photographs: Corbis pp. 15 (© Philip Gould), 17 (© Andrew Winning/Reuters); Getty Images pp. 6 (Image Studios), 7, (altrendo images), 8 (Bob Handelman), 9 (altrendo images), 12 (WireImage/Han Myung-Gu), 19 (PATRICK HERTZOG/AFP), 21 (Sean Murphy); istockphoto p. 4 (© Joshua Hodge Photography); Shutterstock pp. 5 (© Beata Becla), 10 (© Ferenc Szelepcsenyi), 11 (© Luisa Fernanda Gonzalez), 13 (© Anthony Correia), 14 (© Lori Monahan Borden), 16 (© Jack Qi), 18 (© Pieter Janssen), 20 (© Losevsky Pavel), 22 (© Ferenc Szelepcsenyi), 23a (© Anthony Correia), 23b (© Luisa Fernanda Gonzalez), 23c (© Pieter Janssen), 23d (© Ferenc Szelepcsenyi).

Front cover photograph of South African singer Thandiswa Mazwai performing during the opening ceremony of the 2010 FIFA World Cup, Johannesburg, South Africa, reproduced with permission of Getty Images (Jamie Squire/FIFA). Back cover photograph of a marching band reproduced with permission of Shutterstock (© Lori Monahan Borden).

Contents

Field Trips

People take field trips to visit
new places.

People take field trips to learn new things.

Field Trip to a Concert

Some people take field trips
to concerts.

A concert is a musical show.

Musicians perform in concerts.

People go to concerts to listen to the musicians play music.

Different Concerts

This is a symphony orchestra.

The musicians play instruments.

This is a pop concert.

The lead singer performs with a band.

This is a marching band.

The band performs on a sports field!

This is a choral concert.

The people sing together to make music.

This is an opera.

The singers act out a story.

How Should You Act at a Concert?

Be quiet during the concert.

When the concert is over, clap to show you enjoyed it!

What Do You Think?

What kind of concert is this?

Look on page 24 for the answer.

Picture Glossary

concert special musical performance

musician person who sings or plays a musical instrument

opera show or play that is performed to music

symphony music played by an orchestra

Index

Notes to Parents and Teachers

Before reading
Explain to children that a field trip is a short visit to a new place, and that it often takes place during a school day. Ask children if they have ever taken a field trip. Explain to children that a concert is a special musical performance. Ask children if they have ever been to a concert. If any children have been to a concert, ask them to share their experiences with the group.

After reading

- Show children the image of an orchestral concert on page 10, and then show them the image of a pop concert on page 12. Ask the children to make a list of the differences between the two images. For example, the number of people, or whether the musicians play instruments or sing.
- Ask the class to name their favorite type of music. Make a list of the different types on a whiteboard.

Answer to page 22
It is a choral concert.